Clear Your Mind

Stop Overthinking, Tune Out Mental Chatter And Worry Less

Balance Your Emotional And Rational Mind

By Steven Schuster
steveschuster@gmail.com

Table Of Contents

Introduction 7

Chapter 1 – The Emotional Mind and The Rational Mind 19

Chapter 2 – Mental Clutter 41

Chapter 3 – Overthinking 59

Chapter 4 – Think Less, Do More 85

Chapter 5 – The Perfect Practice 99

Final Words 113

Reference 115

Endnotes 118

Introduction

The Advantages of Knowing

To have a clear mind, the first step is to understand how your mind works. In order to simplify something you have to know what to simplify.

Have you ever made up your mind about changing your thoughts? You got washed away by a *hell yeah* feeling and Metallica played a badass rock song in your head while you mapped out your big changing plan? For example, you decided to exclude negative thinking from your thoughts. You followed your plan well enough for one or two days, but on the third day something happened and negativity invaded you. Your head got filled with thoughts like bad stuff always seemed to happen to you, that you'd never achieve anything, and so on.

By the time your negative thought thread ended, another negative thread captured your worried mind, namely the realization that you were complaining again despite your life-changing plans of eliminating dark thoughts. Suddenly, the Metallica jam of the previous day transforms into a death march, and you fall deeper into the pits of self-pity and disappointment of not being able to keep up with your resolution.

Stories like this happen very often with many of us. We set our mind to something, but the same mind sabotages us. A vow to be nicer to our overbearing mother, or our sloppy spouse, or our chattering-but-kind-hearted colleague, gets flushed in the toilet when we lose presence in the moment and forget about the vow. Then we react with usual negativity, and only when the red clouds disappear do we realize that we had another neural hijacking. As a consequence, we start having a fight with ourselves inside our mind. Our mind chatters, struggles, craves improvement, and becomes angry for not improving.

Can this neural chaos be tamed somehow?

This is debatable. The best chances you have to dissolve the chaos in your brain is to get to know how it works. Knowledge dissolves the Gordian knot. You have to know which of these thoughts you should stop fighting against. Some thoughts are evolutionarily coded into our brain, and you should stop trying to change them. When I was five years old, I thought that taking a breath was some kind of personal deficiency, some vicious OCD that I should eradicate, otherwise people would think I'm a weirdo. As a result, I focused on not taking a breath. Somehow, the impenitent crave to repeat the weirdness with my nose came back after a minute. I focused better the next time, but after a minute or so it came back again. I went to my parents crying, saying that I was crazy because this stupid snuffle wouldn't stop. I told them that I tried to stop it, but it kept coming back. You can imagine their bewilderment while listening to me. They told me that the stupid snuffle kept me alive, and I should never try to stop doing it again. This is how, at the age of five, I learned that breathing is normal.

Ten years later I learned that the most primitive part of the human brain that we share with all other species – the root brain – is responsible to regulate breathing and other basic life functions. This ancient brain doesn't think, doesn't learn, it's an autopilot that keeps the body running, granting survival. (Daniel Goleman, Emotional Intelligence pg. 10) My childish attempt to stop the stupid sniffing, therefore, was in vain. Later in this book we'll see that this is similar to some of the fights we have in our head regarding our thoughts.

Which thoughts can be changed and which are those we should change? How should we pick our fights with our mind? Is the fight worthwhile or does it just create greater chaos? Isn't simple understanding more helpful and enlightening? Sometimes simply knowing that what we think about is not wrong or abnormal can give a peace of mind. This leads to acceptance and the mental knot will dissolve by itself.

Recently I learned that having negative thoughts is neither abnormal nor unnecessary. What's more, sometimes they are completely well grounded. If I lived a hundred thousand years ago, they'd be indispensable.

This is why I chose to go through the rudimentary activity of our minds in the following chapters. Yes, minds. – both the rational and emotional minds.

The Advantages of Not Knowing

I get many emails from readers asking how they can shut down their negative mental small-talk. The annoying cerebral chitchat that tells them they will never find a good partner or their business will never hit the six-figure-per-month income. Before you start thinking that something's wrong with you, let me tell you that we all have this kind of self-talk. Even those who score a happiness touchdown most days face diminished self-esteem struggles once in a while.

Reading Mark Manson's controversial bestseller, *The Subtle Art Of Not Giving a F...,* confirmed something for me that I suspected for a long time but never really thought about in depth. People sometimes don't know what they are talking – and therefore thinking – about.

What do I mean here? Exactly what I wrote. We sometimes indeed have no idea why we act or say things in a certain way. Sometimes we are totally calm, but in the next moment we lose it and become anxious, depressed or, contrarily, very happy. We talk about our happiness or anxiety but we don't know why we feel it all of the sudden. (There is an explanation and I will write about it in the next chapter.)

Sometimes, out of nowhere an anxiety crawls into my thoughts about my fragile and awfully young writing career. What if I'm not good enough? What if people won't like what I write? What if the Earth will be invaded by alien cyborgs, the internet collapses and I sit in total existential isolation? Or what if my boyfriend will break up with me when I think he's about to propose? What if my children will be serial killers, or worse, some sort of Justin Bieber? Holy cow, alien cyborgs, Justin Bieber? Where did *these* thoughts come from? I don't know, but maybe it's for the best.

I'm clueless about what I'm thinking about. Who knows what the future holds? Maybe soon I won't even be excited about writing anymore and I'll start doing something different. Maybe in twenty years having serial killers or Justin Biebers is the best thing that could happen because they repel the alien cyborgs. The future is so unpredictable, and we change so much as people in life that it is impossible to predict if the worst outcome of a present fear is a good or bad thing in the future.

Occasionally reminding myself about my own cluelessness helps me overcome existential dilemmas about my future. Whatever my mind chatters about right now is probably wrong.

There is a twist in this story. If our mind is unreliable and we don't know what we're thinking, and our thoughts might be wrong, that applies to all thoughts: negative and positive. People question their negative beliefs much easier than their positive ones. However, both are equally important. Questioning positive beliefs brings you back to Earth, keeps you from becoming over-confident or arrogant, and most importantly, eases your mind.

The higher the stakes you set yourself, the bigger the pressure you'll feel to live up to them. Mark Manson addressed this issue with the following example in his [blog post](). "If I believe I'm destined to be the next Leo Tolstoy or Albert Einstein, that is a LOT of […] pressure to live up to. And that pressure is likely to cripple me and turn me into a neurotic […] (insert the noun that follows "neurotic" since that is an adjective). That pressure is likely to close me off to any and all important feedback. I wouldn't be able to write a word. I'd second guess every single sentence, including this one."

The advantage of accepting that you don't know many things you think you know can relieve you from a lot of mental clutter. If your goal is to have a minimalist mind, the best you can do is to accept that you're sometimes wrong, and that's perfectly all right. The time you invest in self-whipping thoughts can be spent much better, like taking action instead of thinking about an unknowable future.

Why do I say we don't know what we think?

A few centuries ago astrologists believed that the Earth was in the center of the Universe and everything else revolved around it. My people believed in a small, black haired man who liked to scream German words had good values upon which they could build a superior world-nation.

When I was a child I believed my parents when they told me carrots will help me whistle better and with my improved whistles I will attract pigeons. I also believed spinach makes you stronger but I resisted eating it to avoid getting disproportionately large forearms like Popeye does. As a fifteen-year-old I thought it was lame to be nice to others and disinterest was the way to win respect.

When I had my first girlfriend, I believed we'll always be together. When she first cheated on me I thought I'll never forgive her. When we broke up I was certain I'll never love anybody as much again. And for some weird reason I was convinced that no one would love me as she did. My second girlfriend loved me much more than I did. I thought I was responsible for her feelings. I felt a guilty, horrible person of not loving her more. I was wrong all the way through the carrots to love.

I don't believe there is absolute right or wrong. There are things you experience to be right or wrong for you based on your values. Neutrally approaching it, your freedom of practicing your rightness expands to the point where you violate someone else's freedom in doing so. Not considering extreme negative values that people considered right, we can agree that "right" or "wrong" are subjective. Based on different experiences and values, people will have different answers to the same questions. And none of these answers will be better or worse than the other.

Our own answers might be different today than what we had ten years ago. Ten years ago I was convinced that I should be mean to gain respect. Today I believe I was wrong back then. People have a history of being wrong about things they believed to be right. You have a history of being wrong about things you believed to be right.

You have a superpower. This superpower is the ability to think. Your brain works all the time. It has to think about something 24/7. When it becomes puzzled what you should think about a situation you have with another person, it starts to think what that other person must be thinking about. Did you ever caught yourself assuming what someone will think, react or say? If you agree with what I said until now, how can you be sure what you think someone else thinks to be right?

The brain is the deal breaker part of our body that differentiates us from other species. It is, however, a very fickle organ. It makes us believe the most peculiar things. It convinces us that we saw stuff that weren't really there. It can even re-write our memory. For example, a research has been made where people were shown holiday pictures in Disney land where Bugs Bunny shakes hands with the kids. After the picture slide show was over, some subjects clearly remembered shaking Bugs Bunny's hand, as well, when they were in Disneyland even though Bugs Bunny never appeared in Disney Land. It is a Warner Brothers character.

My point with this extremely long introduction is to give you enough reasons to see, it is not advisable to try to guess what someone else thinks. It is not advisable to believe even what your own thoughts are. I really don't want to pull the rug out under your feet but the quicker you accept that your mind should be questioned from time to time, the better decision maker you'll become. The better decisions you'll make, the less headache you'll have from bad decisions. The less headache you have the less mental clutter you'll have to deal with. And bang, here you reached the state you're looking for, the hope you've bought this book for – the minimalist mindset.

This is all good, and you made my heart race with this pep-talk introduction, Zoe, but I still don't know how to get there, how to know what to ignore, make better decisions, have less headache, mental clutter and a minimalist mind, you might think. Or not, I might be wrong about what you think. But if I'm right, then don't worry about the staying in the dark regarding the hows. In the following chapters I will talk about your brain's function, how to connect it with minimalism, how to keep under your control your most annoying mental habits and how to let go of those mental hiccups you can't control.

Chapter 1 – The Emotional Mind and The Rational Mind

Zen Buddhism differentiates two types of mind: the thinking mind and the observing (or watching) mind. The first type is the voice is your head that relentlessly blabs, and even if you decide to meditate and quiet your thoughts, it still will project some pictures and thoughts. The thinking mind never sleeps: it chatters to you when you queue, when you're about to sleep, sometimes even in your sleep. Did you ever notice this? Yes? Then you did it with your observing mind.

The observing mind is the one you should use to keep track of your thoughts and actions. Unfortunately, people don't use their observing minds. Until I read about Zen Buddhism, I didn't even know it existed. I didn't call him observing mind, mostly just better judgment or my right mind. Usually I wasn't in my right mind. When someone cries out to you saying, "What were you thinking? You're not in your right mind!", that person actually means, "Hey, you! Please check upon your thinking mind with your observing mind because it's running wild!"

When the thinking mind gets out of control, the observing mind can't do much about it. Have you ever asked someone for help how to channel your anger? "What can I do to stop feeling angry?"

The answer is, you can't stop it. Once the thinking mind gets unchained, that horse is gone. What you can do is to not relate with your emotions. Zen teaches that instead of telling yourself "I am angry" say "I feel anger". You are not the human form of anger, you just got poisoned by this emotion. Making this tiny thought switch, you'll defuse yourself from the emotion.[i]

The Biological Structure of Your Two Minds

As I mentioned in the previous chapter, the evolutional timeline of the human brain started with the brain stem. It is positioned atop the spinal cord. This primitive brain is responsible for the metabolism of the organs, and to control motion and different reactions. The emotional centers emerged from this primitive brain hundreds of thousands of years later. Later, the neocortex, the thinking brain, evolved from the emotional centers.

Based on this neuropsychological data one thing is clear: our emotional mind is millions of years ahead of our thinking mind. On the yearly calendar of human brain evolution, the neocortex appeared sometime in December. Therefore, emotional reactions as basic instincts are much more present in our subconscious mind than rational reactions.

The first layer of the ancient emotional cells atop the brainstem was responsible for analyzing smells. In other words, the first kind of emotions ever felt were generated by smelling. The olfactory lobe, or as I call it, the smelling brain, granted survival by distinguishing nutritious smells from poisonous, the smell of a friend, sexual partner or foe, and identifying all the scents carried by the wind.

The second layer of the emotional brain was responsible for sending messages to the entire nervous system about what the body should do: get closer, run away, bite, throw, chase, etc.

As the first mammals appeared, new brain layers evolved, forming a small half circle around the brain stem. We call this brain the limbic system. The limbic system is responsible for the more complex emotions as love, hate, anger, or sorrow. The limbic system, as opposed to the previous brain structure, has two important features: it can learn and store memories. Thanks to these features reactions became more refined, more adaptable. For example, if a shelter wasn't safe enough, next time that shelter was avoided.

The last change in the brain's evolution timeline happened about one hundred million years ago, when on top of the thin two-layered cortex (the emotional brain) other layers of brain cells developed. These new layers formed the neocortex which, compared to the old cortex, had a distinguishing, extraordinary thinking ability. The human neocortex interprets what the old cortex's senses perceive. It allows us humans to have thoughts about our thoughts and feelings.

The cortex and the neocortex are connected and intertwined via countless circuits. Thus the emotional center has a strong influence over the thinking brain. (Goleman, Daniel. Emotional Intelligence, pg. 10-12)

Emotions Vs. Reactions

What is the main difference between a long distance and a short distance runner? They have the same task – they have to run. However, they have different goals. The short distance runner has to run as fast as he can to succeed. The long distance runner, on the other hand, has to think about how to preserve his energy, so he runs much slower than a short distance runner, but in a constant and sustainable speed.

The same happens with your emotional brain and thinking brain. The emotional brain is much quicker to react. So, if we say that your thoughts are a 100-meter dash, the emotional brain will run it much faster than the thinking brain. While the thinking brain reaches the target, the emotional brain already had a nap there – if you're lucky. If you're unlucky, it ran an extra hundred meters, giving more trouble to the thinking brain to catch up to.

In evolution the swift emotional brain was essential for survival. In a split second, the emotional brain had to decide if danger was around. If the rational brain would have started to analyze the situation, taking into consideration all the sensible factors to make a decision, you might have ended up dead.

A by-product of the speed of the emotional mind is a strong sense of conviction that follows the emotional reaction. It is not enough to make an emotionally based fight or flight reaction, but you have to be certain that's the good decision to make. Without a subconscious certainty, your mind wouldn't put all the nerves in your system on alert. Emotional decision making and certainty already happen before the thinking mind can even grasp what's going on. This is why you sometimes do something or say something, and only seconds later you think, "Did I really say this out loud? What was I thinking?" That's the thing – you weren't. It was all the deed of your emotional mind, which "sacrifices accuracy for speed". (Goleman, pg. 292)

Social development happened much quicker than the evolutional development could follow. This means that we still sometimes give emotional responses to today's problems that we did thousands of years ago. Clearly, today the fear of getting eaten by a T-Rex is not a real one unless we go to Jurassic World. Whatever fear we sense, in most cases it doesn't threaten our core survival.

Paul Ekman, an American psychologist, and the master of emotions and their relation to mimics, stated that the core, full-powered emotion doesn't even last longer than a few seconds. Everything that follows the blink appearance of an emotion is a mood connected to that particular emotion which becomes sustained if its trigger is sustained. Goleman gives the example of mourning a lost loved one: the feeling of loss, missing the other person, the thought that you will never see him again, it all keeps up the emotion of sorrow.

If you feel angry about something, the full heat of anger lasts just for a brief amount of time. Longtime anger gets sustained if you keep on recalling the reason for your anger. Sometimes you even re-evoke the bad emotion if, for some time, you forget about it because you think you're entitled to express it. Let's say you got angry on your husband for walking in the kitchen with dirty shoes. During the day you forgot about your anger and did your everyday tasks, but when the evening came and your husband got home, you recall your morning anger by vivifying the muddy picture burnt into your memory, and start arguing.

Ekman argues that the true nature of emotions is to last for only a brief amount of time, react to danger with fear and flight response, or feel contentment only for a little while, otherwise you couldn't react to ever-changing circumstances. If our ancestors got caught up in an emotion for too long, they might have failed to react to a new impulse with the adequate emotions and would have been in trouble.

In many cases the emotional brain "enslaves" the thinking brain to its favor. The emotional brain itself cannot sustain an emotion for long, but when aided by the thinking brain, even the slightest hint of anger can be transformed into a long-running daytime soap opera. The thinking brain has the power to keep emotions "alive" for a long time because what we think triggers some emotions. If we constantly think about negative things like,

"I'm a failure," or "I'm hysterical," similar emotions will be triggered: fear, anxiety, and anger.

While we can't control what emotions we feel, in most cases we can choose what kind of thoughts to have. If we control our thoughts better indirectly, we can control our emotional reactions too. We can't prevent an emotion from showing up, but we can prevent how long it lasts. If you want to get rid of anger, you can't vow to yourself that from now on you won't feel angry anymore. This is not how emotions work, and the next time you feel angry, you'll also be disappointed that you couldn't stick to your resolution. Remember the story in the previous chapter? You have to accept that anger, for example, is not something that you can eradicate from your life. Choose your battles more wisely. Don't fight against something that you can't change. What you can change are the thoughts that sustain anger. Pay careful attention to your thoughts that keep you in an angry mood, and intentionally replace them with another thought.

This won't be easy. Do you know the game, "Don't think about the pink elephant"? The point of this game is to keep yourself from thinking about a pink elephant that has a yellow dress and dances the chicken dance. While you read the previous lines you imagined the elephant in a red dress, dancing chicken dance. And now you went back to check if the dress was red or yellow the first time I mentioned it. You're right, it was yellow. I wrote red intentionally to make you question your memory, which was quite easy. I bet whatever you were thinking before, now you're slightly pissed or amused about this experiment, and you are still thinking about the pink elephant in the yellow or red dress.

So, intentionally not thinking about something you shouldn't think about is almost impossible, right? But here is an easy exercise, a switch of focus that if you use, you'll be able to control your thoughts better. Change the self-talk in your head from "I don't want to think about the thoughts that make me angry," to "I want to think about the thoughts that make me happy – or hungry, or horny, or reflective," anything but angry. This exercise might seem like another useless self-help placebo, but in fact it is a mild form of psychological mind conditioning. The brain can think about one thing at a time, and you're taking advantage of it.

When you say you don't want to think about anger, you're still thinking about anger regardless what words you use before it. The main point of the command is anger. As a result, you'll focus on anger.

If you say, "I want to think about happiness," the mental focus will be on happiness. Even if you say, "I don't want to think about happiness," you'll still be thinking of happiness. The only word that matters in your rational command is the thing you want to focus on –the opposite of the emotion you want to avoid.

This is the best exercise you can apply in controlling your emotions. And even so, there is no guarantee about what emotion will you trigger. The rational mind cannot decide what to feel, but it can control the reactions. This is what differentiates humans from the other animal species. If you feel that you could kill your partner for squawking again about the kitchen refurbishment is one thing. You won't actually go to kill her. This is an exaggerated example, but you get the gist. If you can control your reactions in this regard, be sure that you can control them about a much less annoying issue, as well.

Key takeaway: don't fight the emotions, that's useless. It's like a police officer reasoning with a crazy person on the street. Useless. Strengthen the thoughts you give as a reaction to the emotions.

Emotions Are Associative

The emotional mind is associative. As I said before, the limbic system is responsible for storing memories and it is capable of learning. For example, the first time you burn yourself, that pain associated with fire burns into your emotional memory as well, not just your skin. The next time you see a fire, even if you don't touch it, you'll feel certain amount of discomfort. You surely won't go to touch it. Why? Because your emotional memory associated fire with pain, and keeps you safe from danger. In this regard, your emotional memory is your superhero, always saving you.

Emotional memory stores other things, as well. For example, if you get cheated on, it will be very difficult to fully trust another person again – let alone the one who cheated on you. Whenever you see your partner texting on his or her phone, somewhere deep down, you'll start feeling an inexplicable anxiety, and you'll start fighting. You might not even be conscious that you do it because ten years ago you found out about your ex's dishonesty via his or her phone.

Emotional memory doesn't filter its responses through objective reality but through its own perceptions. If you perceive texting as a danger, it doesn't really matter what it is in reality unless you see that your partner is only talking with his or her mother.

Goleman separates two types of emotional "thinking": categorical thinking and personalized thinking.

Categorical thinking sees everything in black and white. There is no middle ground. Whenever we encounter some little bump in the road, people with categorical thinking jump to the worst conclusion, "I never know how to say the right thing," or "I always mess up everything." Do you see the extreme words hidden in these convictions? Always, never, everything, the right thing... They are the main words in a black and white vocabulary. The problem with them is that they can work as a self-fulfilling prophecy. Also, these words give a high level of emotional anxiety. It is very difficult to live up to the expectation of the extreme words, whether they are positive or negative.

For example, if you construct a belief about yourself that you always have to be the best worker of the month, that's a lot of pressure to handle. Categorical thinking in adulthood is emotionally crippling, in my opinion. Regardless of whether the extreme words are attached to a positive or negative thought, it's bad either way. Chill a bit, amigo. The world will still orbit around the sun if you miss that shot, or you fail at a presentation.

I used to be a categorical thinker – big time. One day, when I had an argument with my partner, something clicked. He told me, "You always react the same way to…" I stopped him, saying that he was right, I always reacted like that because he infected me with his categorical thinking belief, gave me a bad reputation and all I did was living up to it, because I started believing in it, too. Then we had a long conversation about unhealthy word usage, and created a black and white words vocabulary where we put all the destructive words we used, and we started to avoid them intentionally. Since then, our disagreements are much smoother and they are "colorful." It's not "always the same reaction"...

Watch your language if you identified yourself as a categorical thinker. Build your own black and white word dictionary to know which words to minimize in your everyday language.

The type of emotional thinking Goleman separates is personalized thinking. People with personalized thinking perceive that the entire universe orbits around them. They take criticism, or neutral remarks, personally. The chair is attacking their legs, not vice versa. The colleague down-talked the color green just because they are wearing green socks and so on. They might seem egotistical, but they are actually suffering from a lot of self-consciousness and feelings of inadequacy. That's why they seem to interpret everything as a personal attack. They have some very deep emotional memory imprinting about not being good enough. Maybe they had overachieving or negligent parents.

Personalized thinkers are the ones about whom we say, "They have a selective memory." This means they are seeking self-confirmation about their beliefs all the time. They try to fish out those memories that support their belief. For example, if they have low self-esteem when they get a negative remark, they will search for memories that confirm the negativity. However, the same goes for positive remarks. If they have low-self esteem and get a positive remark, they contradict it with a cartload of negative emotional memories. Think of that colleague who you praised yesterday on his work ethic, but he gave you at least five reasons why he has rather a bad work ethic.

Selective emotional memory, however, isn't limited to only personalized thinkers. Everybody who is in a highly motivated emotional state is hard to reason with, regardless if they are positively or negatively motivated. It doesn't matter how reasonable your argument is, it won't overwrite temporary emotional convictions. When emotionally charged, people have a great arsenal of reasons why they are right about something.

The main problem with selective emotional memory is that it's insensitive to time. When an event in someone's life takes a similar turn as it did in the past when something bad happened, that person will likely give the same emotional reaction as in the past.

For example, if your partner in the past used criticism to emotionally blackmail you, you won't easily accept criticism from your current partner either, who only wishes to help you. You'll react defensively saying, "No one will ever manipulate me again," and you storm off, or start an argument. Half an hour later, when you think through the circumstances, you analyze that what your partner said was far from being offensive or hurtful. You just stored criticism as something that embittered your life for long, that's how your emotional mind tries to save you from getting hurt again. Old habits die hard.

If emotional memories are strongly imprinted in your limbic system, you'll know what specific event triggered it. Not all emotional imprints are strong. Some are more cannily imprinted in your brain, and you're not even aware that you have that emotional imprint, therefore you won't know when it is triggered. You'll think your reaction is justified rooting from the impulse of the moment, rather than being the manifestation of an old scar. You'll enslave your rational mind with your emotional one to rationalize your actions based on the present moment, remaining oblivious of the hidden actions of the emotional memory.

This is the biological and psychological reason why I dared to say in the previous chapter that sometimes we really have no clue what is going on in our mind. This is why blind certainty can get us into trouble. That's why it is optimal to question our thoughts and actions more often than not.

How to Question Your Own Thoughts in a Constructive Way

Questioning your own thoughts is a form of self-criticism. Make sure that it is constructive instead of destructive. Be specific about what do you want to criticize yourself for. Avoid categorical and personalized thinking. Take a specific thought that needs questioning. Make this thought a significant one, that can clearly illustrate what your problem is and the beliefs around it that need to be changed. For example, take something like the inability to think clearly in when you fight with your mother.

Casting the verdict that you are terrible at conflict management in general will demoralize you. It is categorical thinking. Focus on one specific emotional outburst at a time. Every emotional hijacking has a different emotional memory background. Anger as an emotion can be triggered in many ways. If you take your check-up out of context, you might not find the reason of what triggered the anger, and therefore you can't annihilate it. If you're angry around your mother, focus only on that, not on your road rage – they have nothing to do with each other. Acknowledge what you did well while arguing with your mother, what you did wrong, and what can you change.

To send a clear message about your issue, Daniel Goleman advises to "say exactly what the problem is, what's wrong with it or how it makes you feel and what could be changed."

Harry Levinson, a psychologist, and expert on corporate and organizational behavior improvement, warned that being specific is just as important for (self) praise as for (self-) criticism. If you don't specify a praise you can have false assumptions and build inaccurate overconfidence. For example: if you say "I was awesome" is not okay. It is not specific, and therefore you'll begin to think you're awesome in everything. Say, "I did an awesome job with my presentation today," instead. This way you'll feel contented with yourself at work, but it won't make you believe that you're an awesome partner, father or dog trainer as well. Earn those titles with the accurate action.

When you criticize yourself, be ready to offer yourself some kind of solution to fix the problem. Make the commitment that you'll do your best to avoid that kind of behavior in the future. Without a clear path of improvement, criticism will only cause frustration. You don't need to be ready with five specific examples of solutions in your wizard sleeve, just give yourself a direction, alternative conflict handling approach, etc.

If you get criticism from someone else, don't take it as a personal attack. Take responsibility instead of becoming defensive. If you become too upset, resume the conversation later. Take some time to cool down a bit and contemplate on what you heard. Try to interpret criticism as an opportunity to improve.

Chapter 2 – Mental Clutter

An Overloaded Mind is Less Creative

Did you ever feel like you're only a bystander of your own life? Recently I realized how often I fail to notice the simple pleasures of life. I eat food without truly tasting it. I rush by the beauties of nature, some amazing artwork or a good-looking man (I made an oath to be faithful, not blind) without seeing them. I have a conversation with my dad without being mentally present, and so on.

Why do I do this? I asked myself one day. *Why can't I enjoy the moment*?

It's because my mind is too busy with the future. My thoughts are one step ahead of me, debating about what to do next, and to keep me on my schedule. *Being on schedule is the key to reach your optimal level of success, isn't it?* Not always. I discovered that too much pressure coming from a tight schedule can actually kill creativity and quality work.

There are good things about living in the future. For example, you pass the morning traffic jam much smoother if your mind wanders somewhere else. How do you find a balance? How can one think about the future without losing the moments that are worth living for? How do we keep schedules without pressure?

A study in *Psychological Science* proved that mental clutter significantly stymies creative thinking. Wandering thoughts and obsessive deadlines can diminish focus, distract from what really matters and cause dissatisfaction. This study claims that creative or innovative thoughts prefer to invade your mind when it is clear.

To prove their point, the researchers did some experiments. In one, they tested the power of associative memory based on different levels of "mental loading". The subjects were divided into two groups. One group had to memorize a string of seven digits, the other group a string of two digits. While keeping the digits in their active memory, the subjects had to associate relevant words with a given word as fast as possible. If the given word was spoon, they associated words like soup, fork and so on. As it turned out, those people who had to remember seven digits gave slower and more generic responses than those who had to remember only two digits. The subjects who had to remember only two digits made more creative associations much quicker.

In another experiment, the researchers figured that people who had a higher mental load automatically started to look for the most common response to given questions, while those who had "less on their minds" took some time to brainstorm a more uncommon answer. The study propounded that the human mind, if decluttered, is more willing to search for unique solutions, but when is busy, it will automatically look for the easiest answer.

Is it better to be one hundred percent creative all the time?

No, not really. Evolutionarily speaking, the human brain was set up to act between two extremes: explore and exploit. In other words, sometimes the brain is opened, eager to learn and discover – explore. Other times it prefers to exploit its memory and make decisions based on them. For example, if our ancestors wouldn't have been curious, we'd still live in caves, fighting with wooden sticks. If our ancestors had been overly reckless with a mindset to explore relentlessly, our species wouldn't have survived.

This prehistoric argument is true even today. Being innovative and creative all the time, always discovering, never processing or relying on your memory can be equally destructive as living on memories too much. If you try to stay in the moment all the time, emptying the mind, denying its natural need for chatter will backfire the same way as mental overload. It will tire you and leave you "mindless". It is good to use your memory and let your thoughts wander when you're doing something static or worthless of attention, like sitting in a traffic jam. However, when the time comes, the creative mind should be channeled.

You might not be aware how you overload your brain with data on a daily basis. You memorize a shopping list, some useless website names that you could easily bookmark, names, dates, events...

All these can reduce your mental capacity, leading to slow thinking, mental fatigue and stress.[ii]

Four Types of Mental Clutter You Should Be Aware Of

Steve Scott, in his bestselling book *Declutter Your Mind,* identified four major causes of why your mind gets cluttered. As you saw earlier, a cluttered mind doesn't serve your best innovative interests, and even less your everyday enjoyment of life. Mental clutter keeps you from living the fullest during the special moments in life, like being present when you spend time with your kids, spouse, family and friends. Enjoying the beauty your five senses can capture, like a good meal, nice scenery, an inviting smell, the touch of a furry friend or the healing power of the sound of the nature.

To treat a problem, you first have to identify what the problem is. With the help of Scott's book, you'll get familiar with the symptoms of a cluttered mind.

The first and maybe most harmful reason for mental clutter is stress. Although stress seems to be a natural byproduct of accelerated living, it should be managed and diminished as much as possible. The paradox of choice, the information overload, the mass expectations you put on your shoulders, these all generate stress – but they are all avoidable. There are other stressors out there, which are less easily avoidable like workplace problems. These might be a sickness in the family, the status of the economy and your mortgage, which you can't change, but you still can't help stressing about.

Stress accumulates not only in your mind but also in your, body and can have psychosomatic effects like sleeping and eating disorders, tension in your limbs, or in worst cases depression, peptic ulcers, or stroke. "When life becomes so intense and complicated, our psyches search out escape ramps. Too much input, too much negative exposure, and too many choices can trigger a not-so-healthy coping response," Steve Scott tells in his book.

The second reason mental clutter is one of the stressors mentioned above is the paradox of choice. Getting crippled by the tremendous amount of choices does not only result in form of stress, and that's why I chose to mention it separately. The problem of the paradox of choice increased in the consumer society of the Twentieth and Twenty-first centuries. We have so many options now, so much free information to digest, so many cereals to choose from, so many career options to pursue that every time we choose something we inevitably start thinking about what we missed out on by choosing that. We constantly feel anxious and dissatisfied, brainwashed by the *what ifs* in all areas of life.

We get paralyzed in a grocery store or clothing shop debating what to buy for minutes, or even hours. Our life is stolen while agonizing on mostly unimportant choices, and the anxiety we feel after we made the choice. No wonder that high achievers like Mark Zuckerberg or Steve Jobs fought against decision fatigue in many of their life areas, including clothing. (They committed to wearing the same clothes every day to spare some moments in their life, instead of entering in the "I have nothing to wear" hysteria.)

The third reason for mental clutter is physical clutter. These are actually a chicken and egg story: physical clutter is a manifestation of mental and emotional clutter, while physical clutter triggers mental clutter. If you cut one, the other one will get cleaner, too. It is easier to start to get rid of physical clutter because it is quicker, and has a greater visual impact.

The category of physical clutter is not limited to actual touchable, throwable physical items. Your digital clutter belongs to this group, as well. The multitude of emails you get daily (promotion emails, calls to boring networking events and so on) all radiate a sense of urgency, when in reality they are not that important. It almost feels like every day you get twice as much new information than you got the day before that are still waiting to be processed. Hey, you still have twenty-four hours.

Steve Scott's fourth category is negativity bias. This kind of mindset is absolutely normal and natural. The human brain evolved by coding three mistakes "overestimating threats, underestimating opportunities and underestimating resources (for dealing with threats and fulfilling opportunities)". (Rick Hanson PhD, *Confronting the Negativity Bias*)

As presented in the previous chapter, emotional reactions are out of our thinking brain's control, and are much quicker than rational thoughts. Therefore every little threat we experience can easily spill over, cluttering our thoughts with worry, anxiety, fear and other negative expectations. Emotional reactions can't be modified with thoughts. Only the thinking brain can be retrained to think about something that doesn't fuel the negative emotions more.

One Technique to Release Mental Clutter

As a college student I was a bottom-up thinker. I analyzed where I was in the moment and what I needed to move to the next step, for example, taking an exam successfully. I started to collect data, but lacking an actual target, I often spent too much time learning useless, unhelpful things. In parallel, I was anxious because I didn't know if my knowledge would be enough or not.

Thanks to my college years I realized that bottom-up thinking is not helpful when it comes to personal goals. Without knowing where you are heading, you can easily get lost in the maze of mass information and uncertainty.

When I started my own business, I permanently broke up with the quick-and-easy-but-frustrating-as-hell bottom-up thinking. What kind of mindset did I adopt instead? Top-down thinking.

There are two main differences between bottom-up and top-down thinking. The former focuses on collecting information first, and based on those finding patterns, a solution or goal. The latter sets a clear goal first, which gives a clear idea what specific data is needed to reach the goal. The result of bottom-up thinking is unpredictable, and especially in business life, and unpredictability can cause a lot of avoidable frustrations. Top-down thinking starts with the result and then is broken down to smaller actions that will secure its fulfillment. There is still a risk that the target of top-down thinking will not be reached, but chances for success are significantly higher than with bottom-up thinking.

Once you have a clear target in front of you, the way to get there becomes much clearer. This doesn't mean that you must stick to the target no matter what. Based on your research, your experience as the problems evolve allows you to make changes, but by approaching the problem with top-down thinking you can be much more focused about what steps you need to make.[iii]

The top-down approach sounds complicated, but it really isn't. It's about structuring your thoughts around a given challenge, goal, or wish. Using top-down thinking will help you let go of a lot of unnecessary thoughts. If you make a good plan, you'll know exactly what to do, and when to do it without getting stressed and overwhelmed with options.

How to Create a Good Top-Down Thinking Plan

1. Know what you want to accomplish. For argument's sake, let's say that your goal is to finish a book. (My mind seems overloaded because it chose the easiest example to give, didn't go too creative to plan, let's say, how to get the United States out of debt.) So, the goal is to write a book, a non-fiction book to be more accurate.

2. The second step is to define what will be the key takeaway of the book. For example, *how to eradicate overthinking from your life*.

3. The next step is to do a lot of research on the topic of eradicating overthinking, simplifying thoughts, decluttering the mind and so on, to get an idea of what is needed to be in the book based on the experts' opinion.

4. Add to the research all the thoughts, experience, ideas and solutions you have about the topic.

5. Based on the research, separate the mass amount of data into a logical order and build up ten or twelve chapter topics.

6. Give each chapter two to four key takeaway ideas (A-B-C-D) of what the reader can benefit from.

7. Outline each idea in each chapter based on your research.

8. Start writing the book.

Now, imagine if you started to write a book with bottom-up thinking, meaning you'd start from point eight. Who knows what that book would end up being? If I don't get the result I set in point one and two, it means that I didn't do good top-down planning – or I didn't adapt to changeable circumstances. If I messed up something about the chapters in point five, and two topics have identical messages but I didn't change them, that will make my book repetitive, slow and dull. If I choose not to change the topic just because I planned differently, that's dumb. Top-down thinking requires flexibility to get the best results.

What did I win with top-down thinking? First, a lot of time and ease of mind. Knowing what to do, and when to do it gives the mind some break. The top-down planning of writing a book, by the way, can go on like this:

9. Write the first three chapters in the next X days.

10. Write the second three chapters in the next X days… (And so on until the book is ready. Then give yourself a few days to revise it.)

11. Send to the editor. (She needs five days to edit it.)

Points nine through eleven are the time frame of top-down thinking. Thinking in a top-down manner when it comes to plans can make your life much easier. Your thoughts will become less cluttered and you will save time. I suggest you consider introducing top-down thinking in your life – especially when it comes to your business or career.

There are circumstances when bottom-up thinking can be more helpful, like when you want to create something new and complex, without knowing what the outcome will actually be. From a cognitive psychology point of view, most of our senses perceive information in a bottom-up fashion. For example, the eyes take information from the environment (psychology calls this a sensory input), in other words, we see something. That's the bottom. Then the brain processes the information, recognizes it and turns it into a familiar image, it builds up a final cognition. The same goes on when we hear, taste, touch or smell something. Our sensatory system follows a pure bottom-up structure. This means that all day, whatever we see, hear or smell goes through bottom-up processing.

The individual elements are analyzed first, and then the brain puts them together, creating a larger picture. If you see flowers, it smells like roses and hear bees humming around, your brain will send you the information that you are in a flower garden. All these phases go on very fast, you can't even follow the separate pieces of information your brain collects. You'll just know that you're in a flower garden. However, behind this realization there is a serious bottom-up analysis.

However, when we talk about less subconscious perceptions, like planning how to earn your first million, top-down thinking can be much more effective.

The Clear Plate

I read a sweet story – or practice – on the website of The Minimalists. Joshua Fields Millburn, one of the site's founders, talks about an experiment he is about to try: clearing his plate every time.[iv] What does this mean?

A clear plate in Millburn's understanding means that he only puts only one thing on it at a time. For example, when he reads, he reads. He doesn't mix his plate with reading while watching TV, or reading while running on the treadmill.

He decided to have presence in every action he chooses to do. If he catches up on social media, he gives all his attention to that. If he meets friends, he is all there, instead of letting his thoughts wandering to his mobile and so on. He simply wants to reduce stress in his life, eradicate interruptions imposed by his own or other's expectations.

"I am in control, just as you are—we must remember that. This is my life, I am in charge, and I have the freedom to do what I want," Millburn says. "I'll stay focused on the current activity, and I'll allow no interruptions. I will live my life one moment at a time."

After I read the article, I chose to try Millburn's advice. I focused to stay inside whichever activity I chose to do in the moment. When I read, I let a reading trance take me away. When I wrote, I totally excluded all other distractions. In the beginning it was quite difficult, since I'm by nature the person who likes to stack activities to save time. I'm the one who falls off the treadmill sometimes because I get too distracted flipping the page of a book, or lets her food go cold because I'm totally caught up in a Skype call with my dad. To me, forcing myself to do just one thing was extremely challenging. I thought I would be able to finish only half the things I planned for the day.

To my greatest surprise, quite the opposite happened. I read more than I would have on the treadmill, and I remembered twice as much of what I read. I could eat faster, and the food tasted better being warm. I gave my undivided attention to my dad on Skype and I could set a new record of calorie burning. I also felt much more present in my life. I knew and felt the day's events. I didn't feel like I was teleported from morning to evening in a time capsule without having any memories of the day's events.

The moments in your life deserve your attention. Feeling life and feeling alive is an invaluable state to be in.

Chapter 3 – Overthinking

Have you ever found that you were thinking about a problem too complexly and convinced yourself in the midst of it that you couldn't do anything about it? There's no solution. You can't put up with this problem because it is too complicated for you. You thought you were in a rabbit hole of unsolvable problems so deep that you couldn't find a way out.

Even the most seemingly complicated problem has an explanation and solution. I will prove it in this chapter. The thing is that we sometimes like stuff to be complicated. If it is not complicated enough, we run extra rounds to make them more complicated. Why? Because the root cause of our problem may be too painful, too hard to accept, or it would require us to admit that we were wrong. And today's society is not comfortable with pain.

Overthinking is a way of procrastination. It seems

easier to overthink something and conclude it has no solution than to actually face and solve the problem. "Me? I would *love* to solve this problem, but..." Fill in the rest. Is it out of your control? Are you too old, young, poor, rich, busy, or tired to do it?

Overthinking can be a good way to deter solving the problem, but it is a bitter pill to swallow. The overthinking pill comes with many undesired side effects: anxiety, frustration, anger, powerlessness, sorrow, uncertainty, doubt, just to mention a few. Avoiding a problem to solve will not make the problem go away. It just creates other problems on the top of the problems. Overthinking and the problems it generates make our minds cluttered, make us feel insecure and impatient. Let's see an example of overthinking.

Thinking Overthinking

Joe wanted to eat fries but he hasn't got any at home. It was a stormy Sunday afternoon, the market was already closed in the sleepy little town he was living in. "I will just pass by my friend Sam's place and ask for a potato. He surely has some,"

Joe decided. With the brilliant thought in his mind he got dressed, boots, jacket, hat as one is supposed to dress on a stormy Sunday afternoon in a small town.

Sam lived a couple blocks away, so Joe took the time to figure what to say to Sam when he arrived. He couldn't start with asking directly for the wicked root vegetable, because *then Sam would think* he only cared for that and had no interest in visiting otherwise. He thought he should start chattering about local political issues with Sam to make him interested and ask Joe to hang around.

But it was Sunday afternoon. Sam's wife was probably home, too. *She hates politics, and as a matter of fact, hates me too. She believes that I am a bad influence on Sam. And Sam, the henpecked husband he is, will surely not invite me in, but rather talk like a moron at the front door trying to give eye signals to talk later. But, then who will give me the potatoes? Why am I so angry anyway? It's so annoying. To the heck with Sam's wife, I won't get angry because of her, no sir,* Joe thought as he approached Sam's house, getting more and more worked up.

Joe recalled a few times when Sam turned him away because of his wife – some humiliating and painful memories. "Who does he think he is anyway? Rejecting me like that," Joe grumbled on the empty street. He imagined himself asking for potatoes and Sam rejecting him again. Joe became furious by the time he reached his friend's door. He impatiently started banging it. When Sam came to open it with a wide smile, the only thing Joe could do was:

"Damn your potatoes!" he yelled. Then he stormed away. Sam wasn't entirely sure what just happened. *What potatoes? What's wrong with Joe?*

Joe's story illustrates a wicked quirk of your brain that, if you allow it, can drive you totally nuts. My father used to call it the brain-munching bug, I just call it overthinking.

We humans are the only mammals who can think about thoughts and feelings. This is a gift, but it can be a curse, too. Let's take a common negative feeling: anxiety. You get anxious about an exam you know you learned enough for. Still, anxiety numbs your mind and you start forgetting everything you've learned. When you can't recall something you're sure you knew this morning, you start getting even more anxious. You feel more anxiety because of your anxiety. Now that you're aware that you're anxious, and anxiety makes you forget stuff, you become anxious about anxiety. You just tripled your crippling condition. *Where's the emergency exit of this wicked building?*

Let's examine Joe's story. Joe was hungry, simply craving potatoes. This lacking made him impatient and tense. This tension attracted more and more tension-related memories into his mind. (Remember the section where I was talking about the pink elephant? If you don't want to think about it, you should tell yourself something to think about its opposite, not something you don't want to think about. Joe didn't read this book.) He recalled more memories that made him tense. Then, the fact that he got so angry because of hated subjects like his friend's wife made him even angrier. In his hijacked, petty rage, he lashed out at his friend, who had no idea what Joe was even talking about. On his way home, Joe became even angrier because of his outburst and the self-sabotaged chances to eat fries. Joe is angry at himself for having an angry outburst about being hangry (hungry+ angry). Good job, Joe's brain, you did it! Again.

Chances are, I could risk a very high bet on it, that you experienced similar thought overthinking a few times in your life. Sometimes bitter, sometimes sweet, being able to have thoughts about our thoughts and feelings is a true gift, as long as our thoughts are worthy thinking about. Our brain thinks about something 24/7. When it becomes puzzled about what you should think of a situation you have with another person, like in Joe's case, it starts to think about what that other person must be thinking. Assumption is the death of facts and creates only misunderstandings. Did you ever catch yourself assuming what someone would think, react or say, and then realized you were totally wrong about it?

The brain is the deal-breaker part of our body that differentiates us from other species. It is, however, a very fickle organ. It makes us believe we heard things in a silent room. It convinces us that we saw stuff that wasn't really there. And it can make us adopt beliefs that are totally illogical and untrue. What do I mean here?

Santa and His Goblins

Unfortunately, even though living standards were never better in the Western world, problems like anxiety, worry, anger and dissatisfaction don't seem to cease. What's more, there is an increase in number of them. These negative emotions are a byproduct of consumer society. Today's consumer culture influences our thoughts like no known religion or paranormal belief.

(Please read the following paragraph in your most dramatic, catastrophe-movie-trailer voice, imagining that hoards of drummers are playing a wild rhythm as you interpret each word.)

A new influence was born in the past few decades. Its power spread quicker than anything else before it, settling in every government and public institution, and family home in less than half a century. It has in its power to demonetize nations, prevent or start wars, and drive people to the verge of suicide. Interestingly, this "new God" is perceived and used by everybody the same way, regardless of age, race, nationality, sexual orientation and religion. It has one name as well. It is called *the Internet.*

Undoubtedly, the appearance of the Internet was also the best thing that happened in civilization perhaps since Prometheus stole fire for us. There are countless benefits of the internet, starting form accessibility to communication, information, extended freedom of speech (this is a debatable benefit, but let's ignore the existence of modern trolls for now), mass knowledge, enhanced entertainment, Trip Advisor and so on. Why should someone write a chapter about the benefits of the internet? No one is interested in reading about the good and working things. Those don't need explanation. Now I'll bring the drummers back and continue to talk about the dark side of the Internet Force.

The Internet is like Santa Claus. It knows if you've been good or bad, knows where you are and can reach you to give you presents or punishments. You better watch out, and better not cry. As a proper Santa Claus, the internet has helpers, too. Little minions and goblins collectively called social media platforms.

Here's the problem. These little social media goblins are working hard to gain the attention of Internet Santa. They do a lot of marketing work to be as present on the internet as possible, maximizing their benefits. How can a social media goblin get Internet Santa's attention? This is done by being observed by as many humans as possible.

Let's go a step lower on the ladder and examine the relationship between people and social media goblins. People try to get attention on social media just as much as social media wants to get attention on the internet. Except for a very few "social-media celebrities", most people have zero gain by being "present" on social media. Social media, on the other hand, has a lot to gain becoming more and more present. It's like being rich in Monopoly – good job, but nothing changes in real life.

How does social media attract people? By being attractive. We feel encouraged to share the highlights of our day virtually. Somewhere in the midst of showing-off- my-life-that-is-better-than-yours activities, a new generation of people has been bred to think that anything different than the highlight moments suck. They believe that sorrow, worry, anger, or saying no to cravings is not normal. This is the biggest social problem infecting the 21st century. Look, that girl just got married in Jimmy Choo shoes and a Vera Wang dress, with a giant Tiffany ring blinding the cameras. And that other dude, he just bought the newest Tesla model, directly from Elon Musk. This old fellow here? Just won the lottery after fifty years of unsuccessful attempts. And me? I'm browsing Facebook while cleaning my parrot cage.

And what do I do? Think. Since that cage won't clean itself, I have nothing else to do than think, pity myself, envy everyone else and cunningly plot how I will revenge others' Facebook happiness with mine. What should I do to *look happy* and interesting? A Facebook feed without an at least weekly coolness update is a feed of a sorrowful loser. This is the general perception.

Put your hands on your chest and confess something to yourself. How often did you think there's something wrong with you when you felt like dog muck, while others posted bungee jumping pictures in the Pyrenees?

How can somebody feel normal with misery when all can be seen are happy pictures that, like fertile bunnies, jump around in the greenest virtual field? It is almost impossible not to feel like an oddball about feeling sad, mad, angry or anxious when everybody else seems happy around you.

The compulsive chasing of happiness has become a borderline epidemic. Keeping up with the Joneses physically and virtually makes people feel neurotic, anxious, stressed and inadequate.

What do you think your grandmother did when the guy who didn't become your grandfather left her? She certainly didn't pretend that everything's fine, writing a "Some people who don't deserve my tears, one day you'll regret what you did to me," type of pamphlet in the local newspaper (prehistoric information source), running wild in Vegas to take pictures of the time of her life. She cried instead, wrote her thoughts into her journal, met her girlfriends, discussed that stuff happens, and shortly she moved on without feeling too special or too weird about it.

Notice these distortions of reality. Acknowledge that whatever you see on social media or commercials is just a blink of exaggerated reality. Ninety-nine percent of a person's life lies behind those pictures. Just like you couldn't see it before the reign of Internet Santa and its minions, you can't see it after their appearance either. The only thing that gets highlighted are extremely outstanding moments.

Not only good things are shared eagerly. Think about the catastrophic news you see day by day. Bad news also triggers negative emotions in you like fear, insecurity, anxiety, hysteria. The common thing in positive and negative highlights is their power to leave an impact. Nobody would read about a simple day where nothing happened. That's not cool to see or read about, even though these simple events compose ninety-five percent of our lives.

There are plenty of things out there that we can now see or know. There is a large variety of adventures that can shake up an average life. There are also plenty of things we can discover that aren't as amazing as we thought them to be, or worse, we are not good enough. This cripples our mind and soul. We want to be special so badly, we search for happiness passionately, but somehow we end up being painfully average and unhappy. And we think this is an abnormal state.

There is something that people tend to overlook in the midst of cheesy positivity books, blogs and kitty pictures. Something Mark Manson, the author of "*The Subtle Art Of Not Giving A F-ck*", perfectly summarized, "the desire for more positive experience is itself a negative experience. And, paradoxically, the acceptance of one's negative experience is itself a positive experience."

Does this idea sound weird, inaccurate or wrong? Let me illustrate it with a physical example. Let's say you want to carry water in your palm. You go to the beach, pick up the water and firmly grip it to make sure you won't lose it. What happens when you grasp the water? It starts leaking out from your palm. The tighter your grip is, the more water you'll lose. The same thing happens when you obsessively pursue happiness, coolness or whatever social-medianess. The more you pursue a positive feeling, the less happy you become. Obsession about something only reveals that you lack it. The more beautiful you want to become, the uglier you'll see yourself. The richer you want to be, the more poor you'll feel. The more you crave belonging and love, the lonelier you'll feel.

"You will never be happy if you continue to search for what happiness consists of. You will never live if you are looking for the meaning of life." Albert

Camus.

This doesn't mean that you shouldn't care about your life. You should aim to become your best possible self, but don't obsess on it. Do you remember which kids got a girlfriend or a boyfriend the quickest? Those who seemed disinterested. Did you notice that there are two types of achievers at a company? There are the ADHD, super-want-to-be-the-best people who constantly stress about securing their "bestness", and there are those who are totally laid back, couldn't care less about the outcome and still get the same (if not better) results as the former. The only difference between them is that the first type will probably get a stroke at forty while the second will dance the chicken dance at the age of ninety.

Did you notice that when you care less about something, somehow things fall into place, and you achieve much more than when you grip water?

Why is that? Following Mark Manson's thought thread, if pursuing something positive is negative, then pursuing something negative becomes positive.[v]

For example, the harder you train, the better you'll look. Accepting your insecurities and learning to live with them makes you stronger. Honesty is painful sometimes, but without it there's no trust. Respecting a diet is not easy, but the results speak for themselves. Saying no to someone is terrifying but it gives you time for yourself. Everything of value in life has to be earned by enduring a related difficulty.

Going back to where I began this thought thread, with social media goblins, Internet Santa, and their fairy dust about negative emotions being abnormal. Pain, anger, failure, worry, averageness, boredom are crucial benefits of life. Without them there is no happiness, no personal development. The only abnormality is trying to tear them out of your life.

The best you can do is to be mindful and ignore what you see on social media. Be aware that when you put up with social media banalities, you're racing with a phantom world. Social media with its people and events doesn't have any effect on your life unless you let it. It won't change who you are as a person unless you act upon it. Step out of this virtual loop and look around for those very few worthwhile things you actually care about.

Find the Core Problem of Your Overthinking

Overthinking is born in an information-poor mental environment. Overthinking very often serves to fill in the gaps of missing information with your own thoughts about the question. These thoughts are the children of your emotional memory, therefore they are subjective, biased and past-oriented. To clear your brain from overthinking, be brutally honest with yourself about what you know and don't know. When you see what's missing, instead of filling the gaps with your own thoughts, try to investigate the reality.

Understand your fundamental thinking habits deeply. Rock-solid understanding is the foundation for discovering where the self-sabotaging functions are. Only by identifying them can you change them.

Don't try to rationalize your cluttered thinking with some complex theory. The core reason for a cluttered mind is usually a very simple one. Understand these simple reasons deeply. For example, let's say you become self-conscious when you have to show up at an event that other female colleagues attend. You feel a lot of pressure to fit in, to be pretty enough, to hit some imaginary standard of looks you have. You can construct books full of problems around a simple event, you can be anxious and think for weeks about a gazillion expectations that you have to meet. Sometimes you get so worked up about the main problem that you lose focus of what are you afraid of. In fact, you start believing that your real problem is the dress' color.

The core problem isn't the dress color, neither is the event and the fear associated to it. The root problem is your lack of self-esteem. If you want to dig deeper, you self-esteem is low because you could never feel good enough for your father or mother. This is the main problem. This should be addressed with the adequate thoughts and practices to overcome it. Don't waste your neurons stressing on a dress color. Find out the real deal here. How?

Raise questions. Constantly ask questions to clarify and extend your understanding about your thoughts. What's the real question? The real question leads you to the real problem. It might take several questions to get there.

Getting to a core problem that causes overthinking is like an onion. There are several layers that must be peeled away. Each question answered removes a layer. Clear the layers and clutter as you answer your questions to reveal what is really important.

The only unchanging part of life is change. Don't waste your time not changing for the better. There is room for growth and improvement all the time. Media scholars hinted that in movies the main character is that person who has changed the most during the plot.

In order to find the core problem that causes your overthinking, first you have to identify and ignore all distracting, irrelevant thoughts. Peel the proverbial onion to the core. Then analyze the central issue and search for solutions to handle the mental knot. This all might sound very abstract. The truth is, there is no such thing as abstract. It must always start with something real, and only after the reality core is created can all features of reality be removed.

Know the foundations of your opinions clearly. If you can't explain something, it means you don't know it. Regularly revise your opinions and beliefs. If you think something is fundamentally wrong or right, spend a day assuming that your conviction is true, and one day that your conviction is false and act accordingly. Following this practice, you'll get a wider thinking perspective, you'll be less judgmental, and overthinking caused by the lack of knowledge will dissolve.

For example, if you are a democrat supporter, pretend to be a republican supporter and live accordingly for one day. Hang out with other republicans, blend in, ask for their opinions, beliefs. Stay totally judgment-free. Don't forget, for that day you're a republican, too. This way you'll see which of your preconceptions are true or false. You can try this exercise with other convictions, like religious ones – atheist day switch, a gay or straight switch, or a smoother one, cat lover or dog lover switch.

Become your own Socrates. Ask uncomfortable questions, set yourself uncomfortable tasks. Overthinking diminishes each time you can let go of a rock solid conviction and become more flexible towards it.

The Big Picture

Everything taken to an extreme can be harmful. This is true in the case of thinking, too. Thinking too much can be a very destructive thing. People can think small problems into big ones. They overanalyze, build up or deconstruct meaningless stupidities until the problem grows big and scary enough to run away from it.

Overthinking is harmful even if you do it with positive things. The more you analyze a good event, the less happiness will you feel. At some point any spark the moment created will be vanished by obsessive thoughts. You can self-sabotage your own happiness. What do I mean here? Something good happened to you. Let's say your spouse took you out to a nice dinner. You've been together for a while, so you start assuming he will propose.

At this point, like in the movie *Sliding Doors*, two things can happen. A: He does propose. B: He does not propose. Overthinking related to option B is not hard to guess. You'll start thinking he doesn't even love you, he'll never propose, you're wasting your time, he's not the one, you should break up with him, he wanted to make fun of you by giving you false hopes and so on. If option A happens and all your dreams come true, you can still overthink it: What if he changes his mind at the last minute, what if he didn't actually want to propose, what if he just gave in to your constant pressure, what if he was cheating on you and this is how he wants to feel better about himself, what if he's not the one...

Relax, gal. It's just a dinner. The idea of proposing is the child of overthinking already, let alone all the crazy-ass thoughts that followed. You can see how easy it is to overthink a positive event, which in this case was a pleasant dinner with your boyfriend.

Now you might say, "Yes, you are right. To the rubbish bin with overthinking. I get it. I have to find the root cause, I have to care less about social media, care more about the things what matter... *That's it?* Will I be cured of overthinking if I do all this?"

Why, thank you for asking this! I can't promise that all your thoughts will be linearly wired if you follow everything mentioned above. Chances are that you'll overthink things less and less. Here are some more tips on how you can tame your hyperactive mind.

Put things into a wider perspective. When you feel that uncontrollable mental wave coming to capture your right mind, quickly show it a stop sign, asking: Will this matter in five years? Or five weeks, even five days? They probably won't. It of course depends on the situation. The story of the rude salesperson won't matter in five days. A disagreement with a good friend won't matter in five weeks. A breakup won't matter in five years.

Of course, acknowledging the time perspective won't make the present less painful, but it will help you snap out of overthinking and live in the situation as it really is. You'll be able to find the core cause of the issue easier and treat it accurately.

Accept that you cannot control everything. Thinking things through a thousand times can be a sign of control mania. This deep need for control serves to make sure not to make a mistake, or fail or look like an ass. Stuff happens, it's part of life. You can't have everything under control, you can't avoid failure all the time. And you shouldn't. Failure, and the pain that follows is a natural part of being human. Everyone who you look up to has failed during their lifetime. Everyone makes mistakes

Those things are a part of living a life where you truly stretch your comfort zone. Everyone you may admire and have lived a life that inspires you has failed. They have made mistakes. Nobody got crucified for them. Well, at least not in the past few centuries. Try to see the bad events as valuable feedback you can learn from.

Those things that may look negative today can turn out to be invaluable help to succeed in the future. You can't know it. Today's concepts of positive and negative can easily be reversed in the future. You don't know how yourself of today will think about something tomorrow. The tattoo you love today can become dull and unwanted in ten years. The relationship that ended today can seem to be the best thing that ever happened to you in a year. You can never know what tomorrow holds, don't try to control so obsessively the flow of today.

Negative overthinking, in my experience, strikes the most viciously when I'm tired. As soon as I have five minutes of rest, some unwanted, evil thoughts slowly crawl into my mind. When I am tired, I have the clearest visions about my partner leaving me, my parents dying, losing all my money, becoming deadly ill and other goodies. Of course, somewhere deep down, my thinking brain knows that these are pure nonsenses and I shouldn't even think about them they are so not grounded. But what can I do, fatigue just brings out my worst fears.

If you and I are similar in this regard, let me share with you how I can get rid of these thoughts. I take advantage of my emotional memory and recall the last time I had these apocalyptic visions and remind myself that nothing happened. Why would anything happen now? It can help me if I call my parents or my partner just to tell them I love them, or I go to blend a green juice to secure my healthy life, or change the password on my bank account. All these actions are, of course, just painkillers, but if they help me snap out of my fatalistic overthinking fantasies, why not use them? Ultimately, the best solution to get over overthinking triggered by fatigue is a very simple one: rest. Sleep. Don't try to finish writing those last two hundred words or correct that last test. Sleep earlier and wake earlier tomorrow.

Chapter 4 – Think Less, Do More

When I am in San Francisco, I like to go to a café in Japan Town. It's a quiet, dark little café with an excellent mocha latte and unreliable internet that prevents me from getting too distracted from the book I'm reading – or writing. But is good enough to search for the basics in Google. I usually spend a couple of hours there, and then I go to a nearby grocery store to buy some sushi makis for lunch. After a few occasions, I discovered that I get always the same things. One plate of tuna makis and one of salmon makis.

The thing is, I don't really like tuna that much. I like salmon much more. Still, for the sake of variety I buy both of them instead of buying only salmon makis. If I had to choose only one plate, I'd choose the salmon. If I went to eat lunch twice choosing only one plate, I'd choose salmon both times. Why do I end up buying tuna, then?

For the sake of variety? What variety? Why is variety even better? Do I buy them because this is how I show appreciation for salmon makis? If I only had salmon makis, all of them would be the same, established on a relatively low place my personal scale of worth. However, having only half salmon makis makes them more valuable. You may wonder, "Okay, salmon makis, got it, but where are you heading with this crazy brainstorm?"

Let me get to the point. Having this seemingly useless mental chatter on my way back to the café after lunch made me realize something.

Some of the mental chatter and clutter is necessary to make you satisfied. If you are only thinking about valuable information, you're always on the point, none of your thoughts would be truly valuable. Some unimportant mental chatter gives true value for the good thoughts. You appreciate good thoughts more because they are more scarce, and pop out in your nonsensical mental chatter.

Does the nonsense make you feel weird sometimes? Sure it does. But this weirdness is also part of you. Searching for a slightly less wrong answer through your emotional memory arsenal is not a bad thing. Without thinking about something, you won't find answers. That way you'll accept others' "truth" that will inevitably feel foreign, make you feel uncomfortable and turn on your brain-munching bug of overthinking.

Let me clarify it now. This type of mental chatter does not equal obsessive-compulsive overthinking, or the unhealthy mental overload I talked about in previous chapters.

This kind of inner chatter is the purest, most innocent instinctive voice of yours. This voice has a childish curiosity, a willingness to discover and understand the world for your benefit, not to mess your life up. If you want a visual picture about it, this voice is the proverbial angel on your right shoulder. It's the voice of your true personality, part of those little quirks and perks that make you you. This relentless pure chatter will give birth to some great ideas that take you forward instead of holding you back.

You know how can you distinguish "helpful mental chatter" from that compulsory feeling of overthinking? Helpful mental chatter is followed by action. Overthinking serves mostly to avoid taking action.

There's a weird paradox in our overthinking system. We overthink because if something is not complicated, or doesn't seem challenging enough, we attach little value to it. It's not worthy of action. As soon as we overcomplicate it, we fail taking action, because it then scares us.

Some people know what they are supposed to do, but they simply don't act. Others get stuck in analysis paralysis to avoid failure and pain. However, avoiding pain and failure is not helpful. It fosters people from the chance to learn. Not knowing the future, a failure today can become a great success tomorrow, if you let it.

Ditch the analysis paralysis, and make decisions instead. Whatever decision you make will bring you somewhere. It can be a place for success or a place to learn. Yet, failing to make a decision means you failed to learn and grow. Now and then you'll hit proverbial forks in the road. When this happens, you may think that you have two options, going left or going right. The Minimalists, Joshua Fields Millburn and Ryan Nicodemus, argue that you have not two but four choices when it comes to an existential crossroads.

The first option is what they call "the right path". This is the path of an obvious right decision. There are no questions related to this road. It is like Broadway, surrounded by palm trees, illuminated, and fireworks sparking all the way around. These are choices like, "Should I kill my banker for mismanaging my money or shall I solve this issue peacefully within the borders of the law?" Obviously, the first option is a no-no.

The other side of the obvious choices is called "the wrong path". Choices here are blatantly wrong. If you have a little reason, conscience or sensibility, you avoid these routes. Sometimes they may seem quite tempting, like telling your annoying boss that, "She's an ugly witch with serious sociopath manners, it's no wonder she doesn't have a husband." Taking revenge on her in such a manner is a very attractive option, but you and I both know that you're much better than that.

The Minimalists call the third type of choice one can make "the left path". In many cases one path seems right but so does the other. Maybe you cannot tell which path is the better one. Maybe one would be good short term, the other long term. Like the translation offer I once received, X dollars advance plus ten percent royalty, or no advance but twenty percent royalty. Clearly, for the short term the first option sounded more tempting. Who cares about a five-year-length reward when she can spend the earnings today? In these cases the best choice is to collect all the pros and cons of today for both options. Why today? Because who knows what tomorrow brings. You can't know what your future self will wish. If you picked right, good job. If you picked wrong, learn from it. I picked the second option, by the way, the long term twenty percent. Why? Based on my needs of today, I didn't need quick money, fortunately. Since I didn't know how I would stand financially in five years, that twenty percent secure savings gives me peace of mind. In my case, long term investment was a pro of today.

The fourth choice is to make no choice at all. When we look at two unknown possibilities, we often freeze and start overthinking them, get into analysis paralysis to avoid taking action and failure. Not making a decision is also a decision, but it is the worst kind. It will keep you stuck.[vi]

Why You Shouldn't Worry About Your Decisions Too Much

I could answer this hypothesis with a simple cliché answer, like you are just small dust in the endless eternity of the universe. Your decisions don't usually make any significant change to the big picture, so don't take yourself so seriously. Well, if I was looking for an answer, and read a book that served me with something I just said, I'd be very grateful, because I knew with what to light my first fire come winter.

Here is another, less cliché answer that might actually help your decision-making mind monster. Decisions that we have to make each day are connected to one single frame of time, our future.

As a matter of fact, there is no other species on earth that anticipates future events like we humans do. Squirrels may save nuts for winter, migratory birds might fly south, but their squirrel and bird brains don't construct their futures like ours do. They are simple, driven by basic instinct, and sensing a decrease in temperature they know that it is time to do what they have coded in their nature. They put together present events (I feel cold) with past events (last time I stayed here for too long when it was cold, I almost froze) to "predict" a possible consequence for the future. Their brain doesn't jump to these conclusions based on conscious thoughts, only purely instinctual ones. Daniel Gilbert in his bestselling book, *Stumbling On Happiness* calls this kind of predictions "nexting". What is nexting? It's an alternative made-up word by him to refer to predictions such as the squirrel's nut scavenging habits. Decisions like that are short-term decisions triggered by the here and now. They are not far-reaching predictions like stock market change, the next dominant musical or painting style, or Taylor Swift's next boyfriend. Nexting is a chain of decision-making in the present moment.

Every moment you make a nexting type of decision. Now, for example you're reading my lines nexting about where this thought about nexting is going. It is nexting when you take your umbrella instinctively when you see clouds outside. Nexting is completing a sentence that starts with "my heart will" with "go on". If we, humans could only do nexting, we wouldn't be any different than our canary in the cage. The canary doesn't have any sense about the future, it just peacefully twitters, swinging on its little swing. When it's hungry, he squeaks loudly because it *knows* that food will follow. The reflex of the bird's brain is built upon the angry owner's lack of patience.

We are different. An unprecedented growth doubled the size of the brain of our ancestors, making the one-and-a-quarter-pound brain of the Homo habilis a nearly three-pound brain of the Homo sapiens. Breaking down this growth to different areas, a disproportionate growth affected a certain area of the brain that we call the frontal lobe. This part of the brain, as you might have guessed from its name, is positioned above the eyes, in the front of the skull. (C. A. Banyas, *"Evolution and Phylogenetic History of the Frontal Lobes"*, pg. 83-106)

In the 1800s psychologists and neurologists assumed that the frontal lobe was a good-for-nothing part of the brain which if gets injured, nothing really changes in a person's behavior. Later, in the early 1900s, their opinion slightly changed. Following some experiments made on monkeys, they observed that lobotomizing them (chemically or mechanically destroying some parts of the frontal lobe) they became much calmer afterwards. The animals that were previously outraged if their food was withheld now patiently waited for their portion. A Portuguese physician, António Egas Moniz, tried the method on human patients in the mid 1900s to treat anxiety and depression. They experienced the same effect as the monkeys. They felt much calmer. (D. Gilbert, *"Stumbling on Happiness"*, pg. 13-14.)

As a matter of fact, they were very calm, like not having *any* worry in the world. The breakthrough discovery of the next decades regarding the damage to the frontal lobe stated that people lost their ability to think about the future. Patients with frontal lobe damage seemed unchanged as long as they didn't have to make any predictions about the future, they didn't have to plan. What's common in planning and anxiety? They are both future-related. Scientists today admit that humans without a healthy frontal lobe are like canaries, trapped in the eternal present, unable to "consider the self's extended existence throughout time." (Gilbert, pg. 15.)

The frontal lobe, the youngest part of our brain, makes long-term planning happen. Long-term plans are those that require our attention to choose one of the four types of decisions we can make (preferably number one and three, choosing the right thing or the left thing). I also stated that making these long term decisions shouldn't worry us too much – and not because we're just dust in the wind.

It is because we don't know our future selves.

Your future self is like an ungrateful child. It doesn't matter how much you struggle making the best possible decisions for future you, it won't be enough. Whatever you consider the best for your future self today, in a few years it will seem rather odd or dull. And that's good. It means you grew. You have a wider perspective and you are less wrong about things than you were a few years before.

What I say here doesn't mean you shouldn't choose the best option possible your today's mind can conceive for your future self, but don't overthink it. Take it easy, because chances are that your future self "will know it better" anyway. Do you ever recall some opinions you had a while ago that today seem totally nutty? Yes, that's your current self trashing your past self, who, guess what, made the best decision you could make at that moment.

I was a late bloomer. I truly believed that my first relationship would be the last and we'd always be together, having a vegetable garden and dogs. When we broke up I thought I'd never love again. With my second girlfriend I thought that this love was not how love was supposed to look like, like there was a standard for love. I was full of weird thoughts and decisions that, I thought then, served my best interests. Today I can only laugh about them. When my first girlfriend broke up with me, I was devastated. I decided to believe that I'd never be okay again –I was ever wrong.

I remember how frozen, broken and depressed I was when I decided to break up with my second girlfriend. I thought the sorrow would never cease and I would never be happy. Wrong again. Those decisions that were so painful and difficult to my past self are the best things that ever happened to my present self. The rule works the other way around, as well. Present tragedies can turn into future successes.

Put that frontal lobe to work on the best future you can conceive today, but don't overestimate its decision's effect on your long-term life. Don't overload your mind with worries.

Don't try to foresee what your future self will want. Don't overthink your options. Use the best of whatever you have now, and make a choice based on those values. Your future self may or may not like your choices of today, but your heart in present will be at peace. That's the only thing you can aim to control.

Chapter 5 – The Perfect Practice

When you want to organize your mind, it always comes down to two simple ideas: discover and commit to the essentials and leave out all the rest.

Your emotions are fickle creatures. The best you can do is to acknowledge them. Don't make mile-long plans on how to take control of your emotions, you can't. The most efficient way to achieve peace of mind is to set limitations to your thoughts.

Choose what you want to spend thoughts and energy on. When you have them, break them down to simpler tasks with the top-down thinking method. For example, if you want to make your mom happy, break this thought down to smaller tasks, like giving her flowers, calling her at random times, mailing her the newest Nora Roberts book with a simple thank you note. Focus on these small tasks. Repeat the small tasks and you'll see that after a time you don't even have to think about them. They just become habit.

Choose the essentials, simplify them and work to get the greatest impact with these minimal actions. Have limitations and simplifications in all of your life areas: personal, financial, professional and so on.

Leo Babauta, in his book *Power of Less,* advises to ask yourself four questions about each task you choose to consider essential:

- Will this have an impact that will last beyond this week or month?
- How will it change my career, my relationships, my life?
- How will this further a long-term goal of mine?
- Is that goal really important?

What are the things and thoughts related to it that you can instantly simplify in your life?

The time spent on your phone, and other electronic devices. You know, Internet Santa is very influential. Don't let it control your life. You can also downsize the amount of engagements you have. Fewer projects to handle will lead to less thoughts and worries.

Practice monotasking. When you eat, just eat. When you work out, be there mentally. When you're doing your regular daily routines, focus on them.

Ease your mind by planning the next day in advance. Choose no more than three tasks for each day. Start your day with these tasks unless they are time bound to the evening. Make sure that the three tasks you choose are relevant ones that take you from A to B. If the tasks are too complex to accomplish in one step, break them down into small tasks that can be accomplished in an hour or less.

Start your day with the most important task even if you're not in the mood for it. Once you start doing it, you'll gain momentum and will have broken through the initial resistance barrier. Mood and motivation comes from starting to do something, not the other way around. If you rely on motivation to start doing a task, you'll fail accomplishment every time you lack motivation, which – let's face it – is the case in most days.

Leo Babauta encourages having an open approach instead of following a strict schedule. This statement goes against the conventional "have a schedule and work your ass off to respect it" mentality. Babauta claims that instead of keeping a schedule, it is more important to simply know your priorities and decide at the moment what you should do. If you know your priorities and how much time and energy you have available, this shouldn't be challenging. Being in the moment, focusing on the most important task according to your own priorities, is much more important than completing everything on a hastily made schedule.

The best state of mind is the state of flow when you do something important. State of flow means you lose yourself in a task, and everything around becomes dull and unimportant. Professor Mihaly Csikszentmihalyi, in his book *Flow: The Psychology of Optimal Experience,* states that people are happiest when they are in a state of concentration, deeply absorbed in what they are doing. In this state of flow, people bury themselves so deeply into the activity that nothing else seems to matter.

He divided a person's mental state into eight challenge and skill levels. If somebody has a low level of skill and challenge, then that person can slip into the state of apathy. For example, if you are bad at copywriting, but you have to do it sometimes at your workplace, you'll probably hate doing it. There will be no reward or praising in it or you, there won't be any negative consequence either. What's the point, you might ask.

If the challenge's level rises and your skill level doesn't, your apathy can turn to worry or anxiety. If you're bad at copywriting, but know it is a crucial task to do in your position, you'll be in terror every time you have to write copy for your company. You'll fear for your job, getting scolded or humiliated and so on.

Medium level skills with low to high challenge levels can result in boredom or frustration. If you're a decent copywriter but nobody at your company cares about it, you'll become bored, unappreciated, and ultimately your motivation for copywriting, and the desire to prove and improve yourself, will decrease.

If you have strong skills in something but the stakes are not high, you feel relaxed. If you know that you're the best, but copywriting skills are seldom needed, you won't feel stressed. You know that any time a copywriting task will pop up, you'll hit the standard.

With a medium challenge level and high level skills, you'll feel in total control. The tasks are achievable with medium effort so there is nothing to worry about.

With high skills and high challenge level you can reach the state of flow. For example, if you are Samsung's copywriter, and you have to write marketing text to outdo Apple, you have to pull your trousers up, because even if you're one of the best, you're competing against the other bests. The task requires your best knowledge. You have to put yourself there one hundred percent. This is the area for improvement, for creativity – for passion.

If you want to enter into a state of flow, choose a task that requires your highest skills and is highly challenging, as well. Eliminate all distractions around you. Then take a deep breath and immerse yourself into the depth of the power of your focusing brain. Don't let anything to kick you out of there – no emotions, no swindling thoughts. Use the power of your thinking brain to your maximal benefit. Focus on the task, melt into it.

I'll give you a hint. The first five, ten, or thirty minutes might not be the easiest or the most "flowy". As Carl Newport said in his book *So Good They Can't Ignore You,* and Mark Manson in his book *The Subtle Art of Not Giving A F.ck,* taking action fuels passion, not vice versa.

First you have to sit down, and *commit* to do your best with your best abilities. At a certain point, you might not even realize when flow will capture you and you'll start working passionately.

Don't rely on passion to take action. Passion lives in the realm of emotions, and emotions are unreliable. Commitment and rational decision live in the world of thoughts. They are the controllable ones. Relying on passion is like building a castle in the sand. It is always exposed to external circumstances. Its security is out of your control. Relying on pure commitment to action is a castle of stone. No wind, ocean or aggressive seagulls can break it.

Do you think you don't have high skills in anything? That you couldn't enter in a state of flow even if you wanted?

I was born with natural drawing skills. I never learned it, I just knew. Compared to professional artists, my drawing skills might not be the best, but I still can enter into a state of flow when I draw. I always become better at drawing as a consequence. I quiet my mind, set a high challenge, like a Christmas gift to my spouse, and I immerse in my highest skill. I might not have the best drawing skills in the world, but compared to my other skills, it is the highest. What I mean is that you don't have to have a collection of gold medals to consider yourself highly skilled in something. Whatever you know better than everything else, or whatever you want to know better than everything else is the skill to use. If you are not at the highly skilled level yet, put your mind to work and learn and improve. Nobody is born to be highly skilled. There's always a shorter or longer learning curve you can't escape. And you shouldn't. Life is in these learning curves.

The Master of All High Skills

Life is a long practice session. Everything worthwhile in life requires practice. When I say practice, you might think about some athletic skill improvement or piano lessons. Many mundane things need to be practiced to become better, like communication, patience or love.

We sometimes make the mistake of thinking only artistic or business skills need practice, like dancing the can can or nailing the deal with business communication. Behind these visible or touchable skills there are other, invisible, skills that also need conscious practice. Like focus, perseverance, self-discipline, confidence, self-awareness and patience. They all need to be grown and improved together to keep up with the actual artistic or business skill to comfortably make it to the next level.

Why? Let's say you become a more skilled writer by reading a lot of books, and practicing writing diligently for a long time. If you don't build up confidence together with it, you don't realize how much better you become (self-awareness) and you don't focus your new knowledge to get the best returns, your improved writing skills won't make you happy or more successful. You'll dwell in a lack of confidence, impostor syndrome and you won't have the courage to publish your work because you focus on limiting beliefs. The same practice principles should be applied in the invisible skills, too.

Most importantly you have to practice seizing control over your thoughts. Without stable thought control you can't feel secure, or in power.

Thomas Sterner, in the book *Practicing Mind*, distinguishes the concepts of "practicing" and "learning". "Practice" in his understanding implies the presence of awareness and will, while "learning" doesn't. When people "practice", they commit to the willful repetition of something with the clear purpose of achieving a goal. Practice incorporates learning. However, learning something doesn't mean that you're also practicing it – or you'll be practically skilled. For example, a brain surgeon can't practice brain surgery without learning the theory of it. Knowing everything about brain surgery in theory won't be enough to operate on brains.

Focus on the process. Just learn and do, do, do. Observe (the outcome) and make adjustments (to improve and achieve the desired result). Use your final target as a steering wheel to navigate your practice, not as an indicator of your progress. Stay in the process to master the thing you're aiming for.

Instant gratification has no real lasting value. It's better to avoid it. How many things can you recall that you worked really hard for? Try to think of five. Getting your degree, starting a business, getting the partner of your dreams, getting a promotion, writing your first book, and so on. Now think about five achievements in your life that required little effort. Can you recall them as easily as those that required a lot of effort?

The more effort you put into your goal, the more patiently you endure hardship and challenges, the more disciplined you recover from failures and go on, the happier you'll be when you finally achieve it. If you look back on your hard road painted with sweat and blood, you'll realize it was not so bad. What's more, it had lots of lessons involved, you became a better person by going on, not giving up, you grew some self-esteem and confidence in the process. You'll realize that the road was much more fun, happy and valuable than the goal itself.

"At what point in a flower's life, from seed to full bloom, has it reached perfection?" asked Thomas Sterner. What's the point in your life when your idealized picture of self-perfection should be achieved? If you use the picture of perfection to inspire yourself, you're on board. However, if the utopia of perfection is a measuring and self-torture device, that's a problem. If you can't find inspiration in perfection, you had better learn to accept and love imperfection.

Sterner says that no moment is completely perfect or completely messed up. For example, if you feel you're bored, rushed, impatient or disappointed with your flow-activity, it means you flipped out of the present moment. In this case, take a break and notice where your mind is focused. It can be in two places: the present or the past.

Practice mastering "the technique of present moment awareness." It will bring you an inner peace and happiness that you can't achieve through the possession of any object or status. When you do your practice "perfectly", you're not conscious of this perfection. The only thing you're aware of is that you're in a state of flow.

One example from the book *Practicing Mind* can illustrate "perfect practice" in action. It is to play or watch someone play computer games. These games offer a visual environment to kick you into focused present moment awareness. In the world of computer games, getting the highest score is the main goal, but the game is the real fun. The process of leveling up in the game takes all of your attention. If you take your sight away from your character to peek at your score, you can lose control over the game and the computer will beat you.

Whatever you constantly practice will become your habit. Habits form your character, and your character will shape your destiny. This is why it is so crucial to focus on what you're practicing, to choose your subject of practice wisely and to stay persistent. Knowing this, how can you waste another moment practicing the wrong thing – or not practicing at all?

Decide what you want to improve with the flow level, exclude distractions and start practicing. The more you practice, the better you'll become. Focus on your confidence level now. Observe that through practice you became better and accept it. The better you become, the more confident you'll be. You have the power to practice whatever you want. This is a very liberating realization.

Final Words

I hope from the bottom of my heart you found some seeds in this book that if you plant in the fertile parts of your brain, you'll be able to simplify your everyday thinking. By now you know that emotions can't be controlled, so don't lose your focus fighting them. Direct your focus on your cognitive abilities instead to find easier solutions to your problems, to stop overcomplicating your life, and to live more peacefully in general.

Using the information and techniques in this book should help you shut out the voices in your head, prevent you from thinking with others' heads, improve acceptance and understanding in your relationships, become more calm, and handle (not control) your emotions.

Don't sweat too much about future decisions. Don't care too much about things that don't have value in your life. Don't take yourself so seriously. Question your thoughts and practice what matters.

Remember what Napoleon Hills said: "Whatever the mind can conceive and believe, it can achieve." If your mind can conceive and believe a less messy mental existence, with practice, patience and perseverance you'll achieve it.

Good luck!

Steven

Reference

Books:

Babauta, Leo. *The Power of Less*. Hay House, 2009.

C. A. Banyas, *"Evolution and Phylogenetic History of the Frontal Lobes"*, pg. 83-106

Csikszentmihaly, Mihaly. *Flow The Psychology of Optimal Experience*. Harper & Row, Publishers, 1990.

Gilbert, Daniel. *Stumbling on Happiness*. Vintage. 2007.

Goleman, Daniel. *Emotional Intelligence*. London: Bloomsbury. 2010.

Manson, Mark. *The subtle art of not giving a f*ck*. Strawberry Hills, NSW: ReadHowYouWant, 2017.

McKey, Zoe. *Discipline Your Mind*. Kalash Media. 2017.

Newport, Cal. *So Good They Can't Ignore You*. Grand Central Publishing. 2012.

Scott, S. J. Davenport, Barrie. *Declutter Your Mind*. Oldtown Publishing LLC, 2016.

Sterner, Thomas M. *The Practicing Mind*. New World Library, 2012.

Websites:

Bar, Moshe. The New York Times. *Think Less, Think Better*. 2016.
https://www.nytimes.com/2016/06/19/opinion/sunday/think-less-think-better.html?_r=0

Manson, Mark. Mark Manson. *The Feedback Loop From Hell*. 2016.
https://markmanson.net/feedback-loop-from-hell

Millburn, Fields, Joshua. Nicodemus, Ryan. The Minimalists. *The Right Path, Wrong Path, Left Path, and No Path*. 2017.
http://www.theminimalists.com/paths/

Millburn, Fields, Joshua. The Minimalists. *Clear Your Damn Plate*. 2017.
http://www.theminimalists.com/plate/

Suster, Mark. Both Sides. *The Benefits of Top-Down Thinking & Why it is Critical to Entrepreneurs*. 2010.

https://bothsidesofthetable.com/the-benefits-of-top-down-thinking-why-it-is-critical-to-entrepreneurs-bec7789659a7

Endnotes

[i] McKey, Zoe. *Discipline Your Mind*. Kalash Media. 2017.

[ii] Bar, Moshe. The New York Times. *Think Less, Think Better*. 2016 https://www.nytimes.com/2016/06/19/opinion/sunday/think-less-think-better.html?_r=0

[iii] Suster, Mark. Both Sides. *The Benefits of Top-Down Thinking & Why it is Critical to Entrepreneurs*. 2010. https://bothsidesofthetable.com/the-benefits-of-top-down-thinking-why-it-is-critical-to-entrepreneurs-bec7789659a7

[iv] Millburn, Fields, Joshua. The Minimalists. *Clear Your Damn Plate*. 2017. http://www.theminimalists.com/plate/

[v] Manson, Mark. Mark Manson. *The Feedback Loop From Hell*. 2016. https://markmanson.net/feedback-loop-from-hell

[vi] Millburn, Fields, Joshua. Nicodemus, Ryan. The Minimalists. *The Right Path, Wrong Path, Left Path, and No Path*. 2017. http://www.theminimalists.com/paths/

Made in the USA
Middletown, DE
20 May 2020